This book is all about me, Olly the Jack Russell and my first adventure on the green carpet at Crufts.

I found my perfect family after being left in a cat basket at the gates of the Blue Cross in Kimpton, UK. I was looked after by a lovely lady called Jackie and she told me that my new family would soon arrive. And they did. My Mum Karen collected me on the 31st of October 2011 when I was about eleven weeks old, and I haven't looked back!

OLLY, THE JACK RUSSELL

IT'S A BRIGHT SUNNY DAY

hip hip hooray!

We're off to a show

and it's time to play

It's a loooong way to go
and I'm ready for fun

It's a long way to go

BUT I'M READY TO RUN!

I'm just so excited

I really can't wait

Mum says we'll get there

AROUND ABOUT EIGHT

There's going to be dogs there

There's going to be lots

Some will be hairy

AND SOME WILL HAVE SPOTS

Some will be black
and some will be brown
Some will be happy
AND SOME WEAR A FROWN

Some will be BIG

and some will be small

So many dogs

AND I'LL SNIFF THEM ALL!

There are so many people

strange smells and new sounds

I'm just soooo excited

OH LOOK, THERE ARE SOME HOUNDS!

We're off to the ring

It must be my turn

Who cares how we do

I'VE GOT CARPET TO BURN!

The lights are quite bright
and the carpet is green
Everyone's watching
EVEN THE QUEEN

I take the first jump
and it's easy as pie
Some dogs are quite fast
BUT BOY, CAN I FLY!

I race to the second

I'm quick to arrive

But mistime the take-off

OOOOOOOOPS, a nosedive!

I right myself quick

and I'm up on my feet

The crowd is all shouting

"HE'S REALLY SO SWEET"

Into the tunnel

my mission is clear

Hold on a second

WHAT'S THIS OVER HERE?

This corner smells good

I'll just have a sniff

Won't be a moment

BE BACK IN A JIFF!

The man with the microphone

likes my fast pace

He says with a laugh

"HE'S ALL OVER THE PLACE!"

Up over the A-frame

WHOOOOOPEEEEEEEE

this is fun

There's no doubt about it

I'm enjoying this run!

This is going well

I think it's a clear!

But Mum's busy calling

"OLLY, COME HERE!"

Sorry Mum, silly me

I think I forgot

that I'm supposed to be jumping

HEY, WHAT'S THAT SMALL SPOT?

Into the weaves

one, two, three, four

Look over there

I SPY THE DOOR!

It's time for my exit
and I'm really quite proud
I've just run my heart out
AND I'M LOVED BY THE CROWD

I'm really quite tired now
and we're back in the car
We're on our way home
AND I KNOW ITS QUITE FAR

Tomorrow's a new day
AND OH GOOD GOLLY
the shout will go up again
"THERE GOES OLLY"

Printed in Poland
by Amazon Fulfillment
Poland Sp. z o.o., Wrocław